ROGER WILLIAMS

THIRTY-TWO POEMS

WINDHAM CRITICAL EDITIONS SERIES

1. John Hay: The Complete Short Stories

2. Roger Williams: Thirty-Two Poems

ROGER WILLIAMS

THIRTY-TWO POEMS

Edited, with an Introduction by

George Monteiro

BRICKTOP HILL BOOKS

2018

Bricktop Hill Books
PO Box 1016
Willimantic, CT 06226

Library of Congress Control Number: 2018960031

ISBN: 978-0-9973669-5-2

To Brenda C. Murphy, my wife

CONTENTS

Note on Editing 12

Introduction: Roger Williams, Poet 13

Poems

        Salutation 27
        Eating / Entertainment 28
        Sleeping / Lodging 29
        Numbers 30
        Relationships 31
        Family / House 32
        Parts of the Body 33
        Discourse / News 34
        Time 35
        Seasons 36
        Travel 37
        The Heavens 38
        Weather 39
        Wind 40
        Fowl 41
        Earth's Fruits 42
        Beasts 43
        Sea 44
        Fish 45
        Garments 46
        Religion 47
        Government 48

Marriage 49
Money 50
Trade 51
Debt 52
Hunting 53
Sports 54
War 55
Painting 56
Sickness 57
The Dead 58

About the Author 61

About the Editor 61

Note on Editing

The text used for Roger Williams's poems is the first (1643) edition of *A Key into the Language of America*. I have taken no liberties with these texts beyond dividing several poems into quatrains in accordance with Williams's practice, converting his italics to roman type, and giving each poem a title taken (or adapted) from the title of the chapter in which it appears. I have retained Williams's spellings, spacing, capitalization, punctuation, and—since there was no second edition wherein corrections might have been made—printer's and author's errors.

Introduction

Roger Williams, Poet

It is said that in his last years Roger Williams (1603?-1683) considered no one but himself and his wife to be worthy of communion in his church but, true to his principles, he barred no one from entering his church.[1] After all, from first to last, he was always a practical idealist. From the moment he was forced to flee the Massachusetts Bay Colony and befriended, succored, and sheltered by the Narragansetts (the Indians whose lands lay beyond the borders of what land was claimed by the English dissidents to the north and east), he realized that he was in a tenuous if not untenable position. He was now a minister without a church or communicants for what in effect was a church of two.

---

[1] Gordon Wood writes: "Admiration for Williams the man and thinker by another great historian of the Puritans, Edmund Morgan, knows no bounds. But as Morgan has pointed out more than once, Williams's conception of church is not ours. He eventually came to doubt even the possibility of a gathered church. His extreme separation, said Morgan, 'reached the position where he could not conscientiously have communion with anyone but his wife'" ("Roger Williams on His Own." *New York Review of Books* [Oct. 25, 2012]).
www.nybooks.com/articles/2012/10/25/radical-pure-roger-williams-his.own/

This was the situation when, in the early 1640s, he sailed back to England to petition for a patent to the land that would eventually come to be known, as a colony and later as a state, Rhode Island and Providence Plantations. But the voyage over the Atlantic, starting from New Amsterdam because Williams was banned from Boston, was long and tedious, and with the practical need to get through long hours and days, practical person that he was, he found a way, as Ralph Waldo Emerson, a century later, was wont to offer as general advice, to improve the time. He decided to address English readers by way of an original document that, published in England on his arrival, might help him get official approval of his petition for a patent. [2] He would write a small book in the form of the then still

---

[2] Given that A Key into the Language of America is written in English and therefore aimed at the English reader and not the New England Indian, Ivy Schweitzer is led to agree with Lawrence Wroth when he concludes: "Ultimately, he [Roger Williams] could not betray his cultural allegiance to Europe; he was, as Lawrence Wroth sadly concludes, 'unable to transcend the limitations of his race and creed' (29)" (The Work of Self-Representation: Lyric Poetry in Colonial New England [Chapel Hill and London, University of North Carolina Press, 1991), p. 188. For a detailed and closely argued examination of how over the years Williams responded to his "Englishness" on religious and political issues (at times indirectly or implicitly), see Edmund S. Morgan's Roger Williams: The Church and the State (New York and London: W. W. Norton, 1967). Curiously, however, Morgan neglects to consider how A Key into the Language of America might fit (or modify) his overall argument. Schweitzer quotes from Lawrence Wroth, Roger Williams, Brown University Papers 14 (Providence: Brown University, 1937).

popular sixteenth-century "emblem-book"—a book made up of allegorical illustrations, accompanied by explanatory morals and or poems.

Williams's prefatory remarks on what he had hoped to accomplish are instructive:

> I present you with a *Key*; I have not heard of the like, yet framed, since it pleased God to bring the mighty *Continent* of *America* to light....
>
> This *Key*, respects the *Native Language* of it [country and natives], and happily may unlocke some *Rarities* concerning the *Natives* themselves, not yet discovered.
>
> I drew the *Materialls* in a rude lumpe at Sea, as a private *helpe* to mine owne memory, that I might not by my present absence *lightly lose* what I had so *dearely bought* in some few yeares *hardship*, and *charges* among the *Barbarians*; yet being reminded by some, what pitie it were to bury those *Materialls* in my *Grave* at land or Sea; and withall, remembring how oft I have been importun'd by *worthy friends*, of all sorts, to afford them some helps this way.
>
> I resolved (by the assistance of *the most High*) to cast those *Materialls* into this *Key*, *pleasant* and *profitable* for *All*, but specially for my *friends* residing in those parts:
>
> A little *Key* may open a *Box*, where lies a *bunch* of *Keyes*.

After this eloquent statement of circumstances and purpose, Williams was confronted with problems of execution—the shaping of materials into a structured book with point and purpose. The structure of the bona fide emblem-book was fixed. Williams's three-part organization of his book follows the received tri-partite structure of the emblem-book: 1. Statements of topic (or topics); 2. Observations; 3. Poem. It is the verse that interests us here, for as far as anyone knows, A Key into the Language of America contains the only verse that Roger Williams published (or even attempted to write) thirty-two poems, which appear one at a time at the end of the thirty-two chapters that constitute Williams's book. But these poems are enough to warrant our consideration that Williams was de facto America's first poet. Others have claimed that honor for Anne Bradstreet (1612-1672), whose only published book during her lifetime was The Tenth Muse Lately Sprung Up in America which appeared in 1650, seven years, one notes, after the publication of A Key into the Language of America, in 1643.

It was an autumn day in 1954 that I first heard of Roger Williams the poet and his poetry. I was then in the early stages of my work at Columbia University toward a master's degree in English. Lewis Leary told his class of seven or eight students, in a course in American Colonial Literature, that the poems in A Key into the Language of America should be extricated from that book and published separately so as to call attention to Williams's unique poetic achievement. Sixty-four years later his appeal has been realized with the publication of *Roger Williams Thirty-Two Poems*. Of course, my instructor was not the first one to call attention to the persistent neglect of Williams's poetry *qua* poetry. Harold S. Jantz, for one, had in 1944, in *The First Century of New England Verse*, issued by the Antiquarian Society (Worcester, Massachusetts), called Williams, "the finest poet among the heretics," predicting that, in the words of Teunissen and Hinz, his poems, when more widely "anthologized," "would certainly become favorites."[3]   Occasionally selected poems have been anthologized as examples of Colonial verse—see Harrison T. Meserole's influential *Seventeenth-Century American Poetry* (1968), for example—but the notion that Roger Williams was a poet, as well as a philosopher, theologian or office-holder, did not stick. Sad to say, their appearance in a few anthologies did not establish him as a poet of note. Roger Williams's name doesn't make it into the indices, let alone Roy Harvey Pearce's text in *The Continuity of American Poetry* (1961) or the whole of Hyatt H. Waggoner's *American Poets: from the Puritans to the Present* (1968).[4] *The*

---

[3] John J. Teunissen and Evelyn J. Hinz, Introduction, *A Key into the Language of America*, ed. Teunissen and Hinz (Detroit: Wayne State University Press, 1973), p. 26.   See also, by the same authors, "Anti-Colonial Satire in Roger Williams's *A Key into the Language of America*," *Ariel*, 7 (No. 3, 1976), 5-26.   In the essay the authors quote from three or four poems (along with numerous examples from the book's prose sections) to demonstrate that Williams has a satirical bite.   They do not acknowledge that Williams's poems are the work of a *poet*.
[4] Vernon Louis Parrington, whose treatment of Roger Williams

Literary History of the United States contains one brief reference to Williams, but does not acknowledge that Williams wrote poetry.[5] The Wikipedia entry on Williams does quote four lines from Williams's eighth poem ("Boast not proud English, of thy birth & blood. / Thy brother Indian is by birth as Good. / Of one blood God made Him, and Thee and All. / As wise, as fair, as strong, as personal"). But it quotes the lines for the sake of the sentiments they express, not as poetry worthy in itself. Nowhere in the entry is it acknowledged that among many other things, Williams was a poet.[6] And neither does Oscar Fay Adams, who admits him to *A Dictionary of American Authors* (1901) on the basis of his several books though their genre is not identified.[7]

The exception—and it is an important one because the critic purports to study Roger Williams's poetic achievement—is Ivy Schweitzer, who concludes *The Work of Self-Representation* (subtitled "Lyric Poetry in Colonial New England") with a final chapter on *A Key into the Language of*

---

is both extensive and detailed, mentions neither *A Key into the Language of America* nor that Williams wrote poetry (*Main Currents in American Thought: An Interpretation of American Literature from the Beginnings to 1920* [1927, 1930]).

[5] Kenneth Murdock, "Writers of New England," *The Literary History of the United States*, rev. ed., one vol., ed. Robert E. Spiller, Willard Thorp, Thomas H. Johnson, and Henry Seidel Canby (New York: Macmillan, 1953), p. 60.

[6] Wikipedia entry, consulted on Aug. 30, 2018.

[7] Oscar Fay Adams, *A Dictionary of American Authors*, 4th ed., rev. (Boston and New York: Houghton, Mifflin, 1901), pp. 426-27.

America.[8]   Her opening words—"Roger Williams is not
known as a poet"—lays down the gauntlet and poses the
challenge.[9] She presents a bill of particulars in evidence in
a lengthy note:

> Miller and Johnson do not include any of
> Williams's poetry in their anthology, *The Puritans*;
> nor does *The Norton Anthology of American Literature*,
> newly edited in 1985, which reprints the *Key*'s
> introductory letter, "Directions for use," and
> extracts from chap. 21 on Narragansett religion,
> but excludes the final poem of the chapter and any
> mention of poetry in the headnote.   Jantz calls
> Williams "the finest poet among the heretics,'
> mentions the *Key* and the true beauty of its lyrics,
> and laments the strange fate of the poems among
> literary historians (22-23).   Meserole prints
> seventeen of the thirty-two poems, slighting their
> context but recognizing Williams's unusual "ability
> to evoke the quality of an image, both apart from
> and in complement to the moral meaning he
> assigns it, [which] sets him apart from many early
> New England verse writers" (177). But most critics
> and biographers dismiss the poetry as unimportant
> or artless.   Perry Miller opines that Williams "was

---

[8] Schweitzer notes, in 1991, that "the only full-scale study of the
poetry [of Roger Williams] that I have been able to find appears
as the first part of the unpublished 1968 [sic] dissertation of
Thomas E. Johnston, Jr." (*Work of Self-Representation*, 271.)
[9] Schweitzer, *Work of Self-Representation*, 271.

too turgid a writer to submit to the discipline of
poetry, and his rhymes are not memorable art"
(*Roger Williams*, 55). M. E. Hall says, "At the close
of each chapter are a few lines of simple, crude
verse that sounds for all the world like the printed
sermons with which good old-fashioned stories use
to end" (83); and Garrett states flatly, "Each
chapter closes with a few stanzas of sententious
doggerel verse. Whatever virtues Williams had, he
was no poet" (127).[10]

Schweitzer does notice that "all but five of the thirty-two
poems consist of three stanzas of ballad measure—an
alternating line of tetrameter and trimeter, rhyming *a b c
b*." "The anomalies occur in chapters 4, 7, 8, 30, and 32:
the first two have stanzas of ballad measure; the next is one
six-line stanza of pentameter couplets; the next has three
stanzas of iambic pentameter; and the last poem has four

[10] Schweitzer, *Work of Self-Representation*, 270-71, n. 5. The
books referred are *The Puritans*, 2 vols., rev., ed. Perry Miller and
Thomas H. Johnson (New York: Harper, 1963); *The Norton
Anthology of American Literature*, rev., ed. Nina Baym, Ronald
Gottesman, Francis Murphy, Laurence B. Holland, and Hershel
Parker (New York: W. W. Norton, 1985); Harold S. Jantz, *The
First Century of New England Verse* (New York: Russell and
Russell, 1962); *Seventeenth-Century American Poetry*, ed. Harrison
T. Meserole (New York: W. W. Norton,1968; Perry Miller, *Roger
Williams: His Contribution to the American Tradition* (Indianapolis
and New York: Bobbs-Merrill, 1953); May Emery Hall, *Roger
Williams* (Boston: Pilgrim Press, 1917); and John Garret, *Roger
Williams: Witness beyond Christendom, 1603-1683* (London:
Macmillan, 1970).

stanzas of ballad measure." But the next sentence returns her to her primary purpose with Williams's verse: "The poems are always introduced with the heading 'More particular,' indicating that the poetic form particularizes the general sentiment of the final observation. Frequently, the poems restate in simple language and sharp images the spiritual truths of the general observations..."[11] Unfortunately, this is about as far she goes in terms of poetic analysis of Williams's verse. Occasionally, she will call attention to an internal rhyme ('*In* wilderness, *in great distress*,' for example), but she does so because it "heightens the implication developed throughout the *Key* of a moral and spiritual as well as a physical wilderness."[12] Her interest in the poetry is always in its meaning, that is, how it contributes to her understanding of Williams's large intentions and purposes, and not, unfortunately for our purposes, in *how* it means.[13]

Thus, oddly, even when a poet acknowledges that Roger Williams might also be seen to be a bona fide poet in his own right, nothing further is made of such recognition. Take, for instance, a more recent work, Rosemarie

---

[11] Schweitzer, *Work of Self-Representation*, 196. See also 208-10.

[12] Schweitzer, *Work of Self-Representation*, 206.

[13] Schweitzer's practice of limiting her reading of Williams's poems to their function as enhancements of meanings already stated in Williams's prose carries over into *The Literatures of Colonial America*, an anthology edited by Schweitzer and Susan Castillo (Malden, Massachusetts, and London: Blackwell Publishers, 2001). What is said about the poems is merely that they are "short" and "emblematic" (268).

Waldrop's 1994 book of poetry titled, boldly, *A Key Into the Language of America*. She points out that Williams ends each of the *Key*'s thirty-two chapters with an original "poem," but chooses not to reproduce his poems, replacing Williams's poems with her own.[14]

It is my hope that the publication of *Roger Williams Thirty-Two Poems* will free Williams's verse from its subservience as merely items in a series of concluding verbal illustrations of points made elsewhere in *A Key into the Language of America*. It offers the reader a Roger Williams who, among other things, is a genuine poet in his own right. His poetic canon—thirty-two poems, written over the span of a few weeks as he crossed the ocean before landing in England at the end of 1642—is presented here in the order in which the poems appear in *A Key into the Language of America*. I like to think they offer a key to the multitudes they contain. Begin, say, with "The Dead,"

---

[14] Waldrop does quote "Salutation" in her introduction but limits herself to the observation that the poem gives emphasis to a point already made in the prose at the expense of the English vis-à-vis the Indian (*A Key Into the Language of America* [New York: New Directions, 1994], p. xvi). Oddly though, several of Williams's poems are available on the net in *Poetry Nook* ("Poetry for Every Occasion"): www.poetrynook.com/poet,roger-williams.) See also Thomas E. Johnston, Jr., "American Puritan Poetic Voices: Essays on Anne Bradstreet, Edward Taylor, Roger Williams, and Philip Pain" (Ph.D. dissertation, Ohio University, 1969), and his essay, "A Note on the Voices of Anne Bradstreet, Edward Taylor, Roger Williams, and Philip Pain," *Early American Literature*, 3 (Fall 1968), 125-26.

which is the last poem in A *Key into the Language of America*
and of this collection. Williams intends always to inform
and persuade the common English reader and hence he
demonstrates (by implication) his disdain for "poetic"
language and imagery. His language here (as everywhere
else in his poetry) is direct, simple and unpoetic ("Bodie
rots," for example, and "False Christ, false Christians"). It
is always in the service of demonstrating the Indian's
sterling spirituality when compared to the English who
falsely protest too much when living but are destined to
face full exposure at the last bar with their Maker.

The Indians say their bodies die,
Their soules they doe not die;
Worse are then Indians such, as hold
The soules mortalitie.

Our hopeless Bodie rots, say they,
Is gone eternally,
English hope better, yet some's hope
Proves endlesse miserie.

Two Worlds of men shall rise and stand
'Fore Christs most dreadfull barre;
Indians, and English naked too,
That now most gallant are.

True Christ most Glorious then shall make
New Earth, and Heavens New;
False Christs, false Christians then shall quake,

O blessed then the True.
This is a text that recalls the certainty of a final judgment
for saint and sinner alike—suggesting a "fire-and-brimstone"
destiny for the "false Christian," but doing so poetically
without naming it as such. Let's now look at a second
poem.

> God makes a Path, provides a Guide,
> And feeds in Wildernesse!
> His glorious Name while breath remaines,
> O that I may confesse.
>
> Lost many a time, I have had no Guide,
> No House, but hollow Tree!
> In stormy Winter night no Fire,
> No Food, no Company:
>
> In him I have found a House, a Bed,
> A Table, Company:
> No Cup so bitter, but's made sweet,
> When God shall Sweetning be.

This poem focuses on one of the great themes of Roger
Williams's poetry: mankind's relationship to a merciful
Christian God. (Williams's other major theme, of course,
is the comparison of the New England Indian with the
Englishman in London, invariably to the latter's
disadvantage.) This poem, beginning "God makes a Path,"
is fostered by the Twenty-third Psalm. Like the King James
rendering of the Psalm,[15] Williams's poem is made out of

basic, ordinary, down-to-earth words heightened to poetry by their usage and in their gathering. Moreover, antecedent in this way to examples offered by John Bunyan and Wordsworth, or, even later, William Carlos Williams, these words, employed in a poetic context, make Roger Williams's lines exemplary and foundational as constituting the earliest poem in the American tradition of the "setting-out" poem, a tradition carried on in, say, Walt Whitman's "The Song of the Open Road" and extended in Robert Frost's "The Road Not Taken." As Roger Williams reminded his English readers, each mortal life takes on the form of a journey, a journey taken under the watchful eye of the Other, working, sometimes, through the efforts of other mortals.

The argument of these poems was not "new," but their "poetry" was.

---

[15] By contrast, *The Bay Psalm Book* version of the Twenty-Third Psalm is florid in its diction and traditional in its crabbed "poetic" syntax. *The Bay Psalm Book* was first printed by Stephen Daye in New England in 1640.

POEMS

Salutation

The Courteous Pagan shall condemne
Uncourteous Englishmen,
Who live like Foxes, Beares and Wolves,
Or Lyon in his Den.

Let none sing blessings to their soules,
For that they Courteous are:
The wild Barbarians with no more
Then Nature, goe so farre:

If Natures Sons both wild and tame,
Humane and Courteous be:
How ill becomes it Sonnes of God
To want Humanity?

Eating / Entertainment

Course bread and water's most their fare;
O Englands diet fine;
Thy cup runs ore with plenteous store
Of wholesome beare and wine.

Sometimes God gives them Fish or Flesh,
Yet they're content without;
And what comes in, they part to friends
And strangers round about.

Gods providence is rich to his,
Let none distrustfull be;
In wildernesse, in great distresse,
These Ravens have fed me.

Sleeping / Lodging

God gives them sleep on Ground, on Straw,

On Sedgie Mats or Boord:

When English softest Beds of Downe,

Sometimes no sleep affoord.

I have knowne them leave their House and
    Mat

To lodge a Friend or stranger,

When Jewes and Christians oft have sent

Christ Jesus to the Manger.

'Fore day they invocate their Gods,

Though Many, False and New:

O how should that God worshipt be,

Who is but One and True?

Numbers

Their Braines are quick, their hands,
Their feet, their tongues, their eyes:
God may fit objects in his time,
To those quicke faculties.

Objects of higher nature make them tell,
The holy number of his Sons Gospel:
Make them and us to tell what told may be;
But stand amazed at Eternitie.

Relationships

The Pagans wild confesse the bonds
Of married chastity:
How vile are Nicolâtians that hold
Of Wives communitie?

How kindly flames of nature burne
In wild humanitie?
Naturall affections who wants, is sure
Far from Christianity.

Best nature's vaine, he's blest that's made
A new and rich partaker
Of divine Nature of his God,
And blest eternall Maker.

Family / House

How busie are the sonnes of men?

How full their heads and hands?

What noyse and tumults in our owne,

And eke in Pagan lands?

Yet I have found lesse noyse, more peace

In wilde America,

Where women quickly build the house,

And quickly move away.

English and Indians busie are,

In parts of their abode:

Yet both stand idle, till God's call

Set them to worke for God.   { Mat. 20.7.

Parts of the Body

Boast not proud English, of thy birth &
    blood,
Thy brother Indian is by birth as Good.
Of one blood God made Him, and Thee &
    All,
As wise, as faire, as strong, as personall.

By nature wrath's his portiõ, thine no more
Till Grace his soule and thine in Christ
    restore,
Make sure thy second birth, else thou shalt
    see,
Heaven ope to Indians wild, but shut to
    thee.

Discourse / News

Mans restlesse soule hath restlesse eyes
    and eares
Wanders in change of sorrows, cares and
    feares.
Faine would it (Bee-like) suck by the ears,
    by the eye
Something that might his hunger satisfie:
The Gospel, or Glad tidings onely can,
Make glad the English, and the Indian.

Time

The Indians find the Sun so sweet,
He is a God they say;
Giving them Light, and Heat, and Fruit,
And Guidance all the day.

They have no helpe of Clock or Watch,
And Sunne they overprize.
Having those artificiall helps, the Sun,
We unthankfully despise,

God is a Sunne and Shield,
A thousand times more bright
Indians, or English, though they see,
Yet how few prise his Light?

Seasons

The Sun and Moone and Stars doe preach,
The Dayes and Nights found out:
Spring, Summer, Fall, and Winter eke
Each Moneth and Yeere about.

So that the wildest sonnes of men
Without excuse shall say,
God's righteous sentence past on us,
(In dreadfull Judgement day.)

If so, what doome is theirs that see,
Not onely Natures light;
But Sun of Rightousnesse, yet chose
To live in darkest Night?

Travel

God makes a Path, provides a Guide,
And feeds in Wildernesse!
His glorious Name while breath remaines,
O that I may confesse.

Lost many a time, I have had no Guide,
No House, but hollow Tree!
In stormy Winter night no Fire,
No Food, no Company:

In him I have found a House, a Bed,
A Table, Company:
No Cup so bitter, but's made sweet,
When God shall Sweet'ning be.

The Heavens

When Sun doth rise the Starres doe set,
Yet there's no need of Light,
God shines a Sunne most glorious,
When Creatures all are Night.

The very Indian Boyes can give,
To many Starres their name,
And know their Course and therein doe,
Excell the English tame.

English and Indians none enquire,
Whose hand these Candles hold;
Who gives these Stars their Names
     himself.   {Job. 35.
More bright ten thousand fold.

Weather

English and Indians spie a Storme,

And seeke a hiding place:

O hearts of stone that thinke and dreame,

Th' everlasting stormes t'out-face.

Proud filthy Sodome saw the Sunne,

Shine or'e her head most bright.

The very day that turn'd she was

To stincking heaps, 'fore night.

How many millions now alive,

Within few yeeres shall rot?

O blest that Soule, whose portion is,

That Rocke that changeth not.

Wind

English and Indian both observe,
The various blasts of wind:
And both I have heard in dreadfull stormes
Cry out aloud, I have sinn'd.

But when the stormes are turn'd to calmes,
And seas grow smooth and still:
Both turne (like Swine) to wallow in,
The filth of former will.

'Tis not a storme on sea, or shore,
'Tis not the Word that can;
But 'tis the Spirit or Breath of God
That must renew the man.

Fowl

If Birds that neither sow nor reape,
Nor store up any food,
Constantly find to them and theirs
A maker kind and Good!

If man provide eke for his Birds,
In Yard, in Coops, in Cage.
And each Bird spends in songs and Tunes,
His little time and Age!

What care will Man, what care will God,
For's wife and Children take?
Millions of birds and Worlds will God.
Sooner then His forsake.

Earth's Fruits

Yeeres thousands since, God gave command
(As we in Scripture find)
That Earth and Trees & Plants should
   bring
Forth fruits each in his kind.

The Wildernesse remembers this,
The wild and howling land
Answers the toyling labour of,
The wildest Indians hand.

But man forgets his Maker, who
Fram'd him in Righteousnesse,
A paradise in Paradise, now worse
Then Indian Wildernesse.

Beasts

The Indians, Wolves, yea, Dogs and Swine,
I have knowne the Deere devoure;
Gods children are sweet prey to all;
But yet the end proves sowre.

For though Gods children lose their lives,
They shalt not loose an haire;
But shall arise, and judge all those,
That now their Judges are.

New-England's wilde beasts are not fierce,
As other wild beasts are:
Some men are not so fierce, and yet
From mildnesse are they farre.

Sea

They see God's wonders that are call'd
Through dreadfull Seas to passe,
In tearing winds and roaring seas,
And calmes as smoothe as glasse.

I have in Europes ships, oft been
In King of terrours hand;
When all have cri'd, Now, now we sinck,
Yet God brought safe to land.

Alone 'mongst Indians in Canoes,
Sometimes o're-turn'd, I have been
Halfe inch from death, in Ocean deepe,
Gods wonders I have seene.

Fish

What Habacuck once spake, mine eyes
Have often seene most true,
The greater fishes devoure the lesse,
And cruelly pursue.

Forcing them through Coves and Creekes,
To leape on driest sand,
To gaspe on earthie element, or die
By wildest Indians hand.

Christs little ones must hunted be
Devour'd; yet rise as Hee.
And eate up those which now a while
Their fierce devourers be.

Garments

O what a Tyrant's Custome long,
How doe men make a tush,
At what's in use, though ne're so fowle:
Without once shame or blush?

Many thousand proper Men and Women,
I have seen met in one place:
Almost all naked, yet not one,
Thought want of clothes disgrace.

Israell was naked, wearing cloathes!
The best clad English-man,   {Exod. 32.
Not cloth'd with Christ, more naked is:
Then naked Indian.

Religion

Two sorts of men shall naked stand.

Before the burning ire   {2 Thes.1.8.

Of him that shortly shall appeare,

In dreadfull flaming fire.

First, millions know not God, nor for

His knowledge, care to seeke:

Millions have knowledge store, but in

Obedience are not meeke.

If woe to Indians, Where shall Turk,

Where shall appeare the Jew?

O, where shall stand the Christian false?

O blessed then the True.

Government

Adulteries, Murthers, Robberies, Thefts,
Wild Indians punish these!
And hold the Scales of Justice so,
That no man farthing leese.

When Indians heare the horrid filths,
Of Irish, English Men,
The horrid Oaths and Murthers late,
Thus say these Indians then.

We weare no Cloaths, have many Gods,
And yet our sinnes are lesse:
You are Barbarians, Pagans wild,
Your Land's the Wildernesse.

Marriage

When Indians heare that some there are
(That Men the Papists call)
Forbidding Mariage Bed and yet,
To thousand Whoredomes fall:

They aske if such doe goe in Cloaths,
And whether God they know?
And when they heare they're richly clad,
Know God, yet practice so.

No sure they're Beasts not men (say they,)
Mens shame and soule disgrace,
Or men have mixt with Beasts and so,
Brought forth that monstrous Race.

Money

The Indians prize not English gold,
Nor English Indians shell:
Each in his place will passe for ought,
What ere men buy or sell.

English and Indians all passe hence,
To an eternall place,
Where shels nor finest gold's worth ought,
Where nought's worth ought but Grace.

This Coyne the Indians know not of,
Who knowes how soone they may?
The English knowing, prize it not,
But fling't like drosse away.

Trade

Oft have I heard these Indians say,
These English will deceive us.
Of all that's ours, our lands and lives.
In th' end they will bereave us.

So say they, whatsoever they buy,
(Though small) which shewes they're shie
Of strangers, fearefull to be catcht
By fraud, deceipt, or lie.

Indians and English feare deceits,
Yet willing both to be
Deceiv'd and couzen'd of precious soule,
Of heaven, Eternitie.

Debt

I have heard ingenuous Indians say,
In debts, they could not sleepe.
How far worse are such English then,
Who love in debts to keepe?

If debts of pounds cause restlesse nights
In trade with man and man,
How hard's that heart the millions owes
To God, and yet sleepe can?

Debts paid, sleep's sweet, sins paid, death's
     sweet,
Death's night then's turn'd to light;
Who dies in sinnes unpaid, that soule
His light's eternall night.

Hunting

Great pains in hunting th' Indians Wild,
And eke the English tame,
Both take, in woods and forrests thicke,
To get their precious game.

Pleasure and Profit, Honour false,
(The World's great Trinitie)
Drive all men through all wayes, all, times,
All weathers, wet and drie.

Pleasure and Profits Honour, sweet,
Eternall, sure and true,
Laid up in God, with equall paines;
Who seekes, who doth pursue?

Sports

Our English Gamesters scorne to stake
Their clothes as Indians do,
Nor yet themselves, alas, yet both
Stake soules and lose them to.

O fearfull Games! the divell stakes
But Strawes and Toyes and Trash,
(For what is All, compar'd with Christ,
But *Dogs meat and Swines wash?)

                    * Phil. 3.8.

Man stakes his Jewell-darling soule,
(His owne most wretched foe)
Ventures, and loseth all in sport
At one most dreadfull throw.

War

The Indians count of Men as Dogs,
It is no Wonder then:
They teare out one anothers throats!
But now that English Men,

That boast themselves Gods Children, and
Members of Christ to be,
That they should thus break out in flames,
Sure 'tis a Mystery!

The second sea'ld Mystery or red Horse,
Whose Rider hath power and will,{ Rev. 2.6.
To take away Peace from Earthly Men,
They must Each other kill.

Painting

Truth is a Native, naked Beauty; but
Lying Inventions are but Indian Paints,
Dissembling hearts their Beautie's but a
    Lye,
Truth is the proper Beauty of Gods Saints.

Fowle are the Indians Haire and painted
    Faces,
More foule such Haire, such Face in Israel.
England so calls her selfe, yet there's
Absoloms foule Haire and Face of Jesabell.

Paints will not bide Christs washing
    Flames of fire,
Fained Inventions will not bide such
    stormes:
O that we may prevent him, that betimes,
Repentance Teares may wash of all such
    Formes.

Sickness

One step twix't Me and Death, (twas
      Davids speech,)
And true of sick Folks all:
Man's Leafe it fades, his Clay house cracks;
Before it's dreadfull Fall.

Like Grashopper the Indian leapes,
Till blasts of sicknesse rise;
Nor soule nor Body Physick hath,
Then Soule and Body dies.

A happy English who for both,
Have precious physicks store:
How should when Christ hath both
      refresh't,
Thy love and zeale be more?

The Dead

The Indians say their bodies die,
Their soules they doe not die;
Worse are then Indians such, as hold
The soules mortalitie.

Our hopeless Bodie rots, say they,
Is gone eternally,
English hope better, yet some's hope
Proves endlesse miserie.

Two Worlds of men shall rise and stand
'Fore Christs most dreadfull barre;
Indians, and English naked too,
That now most gallant are.

True Christ most Glorious then shall make
New Earth, and Heavens New;
False Christs, false Christians then shall
        quake,
O blessed then the True.

About the Author

Roger Williams (c. 1603–1683) is best known for his advocacy of religious tolerance and the separation of church and state, his opposition to the confiscation of land from Native Americans by the Massachusetts Bay Colony, and his founding of the State of Rhode Island after he was banished from Massachusetts. His *Key into the Language of America*, published in London in 1643, was the first study of an Amerindian language in English and brought Europe's attention to Native American language and culture.

About the Editor

George Monteiro, Professor Emeritus of English and American Literature at Brown University, has published essays and books on poets such as Edward Taylor, Emily Dickinson, Robert Frost, Fernando Pessoa, and Elizabeth Bishop, among others. He has translated the poetry of Jorge de Sena, Fernando Pessoa, Pedro da Silveira, and Miguel Torga. He is the author of four books of poetry—*The Coffee Exchange, Double Weaver's Knot, The Pessoa Chronicles: Poems, 1980-2016,* and *As the Crow Flies.*